www.bigidea.com

Zonder**kidz**™

The children's group of Zondervan
www.zonderkidz.com

Even Fish Slappers Need a Second Chance
Copyright © 2002 by Big Idea Productions, Inc.

Requests for information should be addressed to:
Zonderkidz: Grand Rapids, Michigan 49530

ISBN: 0-310-70461-8

Written by: Eric Metaxas
Editor: Cindy Kenney and Gwen Ellis
Cover and Interior Illustrations: Greg Hardin and Robert Vann
Cover Design and Art Direction: Paul Conrad, Karen Poth and Jody Langley
Interior design: Holli Leegwater and Karen Poth

CIP applied for
Printed in United States

02 03 04 05/WP/5 4 3 2 1

BIG IDEA
BOOKS

Even Fish Slappers Need a Second Chance

Written by
Eric Metaxas

Illustrated by
Greg Hardin & Robert Vann

Zonder**kidz**

A long time ago... in a faraway land,
was a city that had gotten way out of hand.
The people who lived there had no shame,
and NINEVEH was that poor city's name.

Why, they'd slap each other with big smelly fishes!
They'd roll in piles of dirty old dishes!

They'd squirt the insides out of knishes! —

AND DID I MENTION THE SLAPPING WITH THE FISHES?

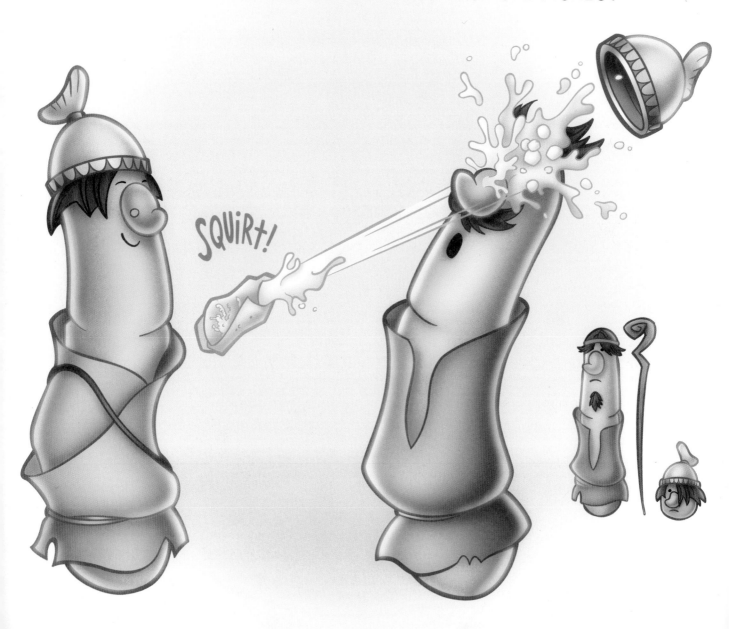

They were nasty and naughty and downright mean
They were wicked and cruel and quite unclean!

They were not very kind. In fact they were rotten!
Do you think that they knew how bad they had gotten?

They'd tickle each other with slippery eels,
They'd throw around banana peels.

They'd tangle up their fishing reels,
They'd eat huge snacks and skip their meals!
They'd quibble and quabble and bibble and babble,
And if it were wrong, they'd dibble and dabble!

And when they ate Italian food,
They'd get EXTRAVAGANTLY crude!

They'd throw their meatballs
through the air!
They'd comb spaghetti
through their hair!

They even made
some terrible wishes!
— AND DID I MENTION
THAT SLAPPING WITH FISHES?

And if all that was NOT enough,
they always acted super tough.
And also very, very rude.
They had a lousy attitude!

NOW... SOME bad things they didn't do.
But those were very, VERY few.

So God sent Jonah, a prophet of old.

With a message from him that was clear and bold.

With a pat on the back and a push from above,

Jonah went to share God's love.

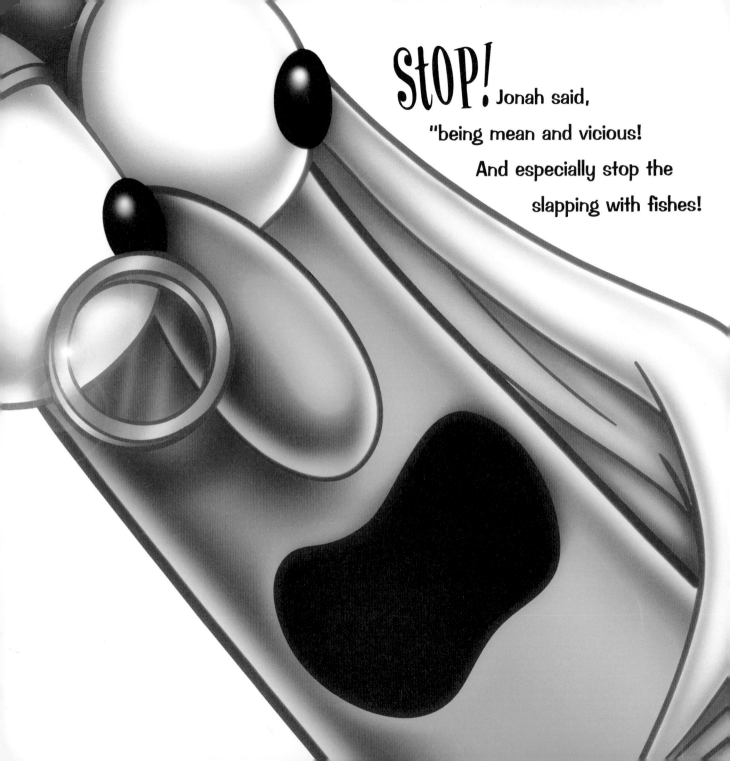

STOP! Jonah said,
"being mean and vicious!
And especially stop the
slapping with fishes!

"Stop your grumbling! And clean your dishes.
This is what the Lord God wishes!"

"Perhaps he's right!" they came to think.

"Perhaps, like fish, we kind of... STINK!"

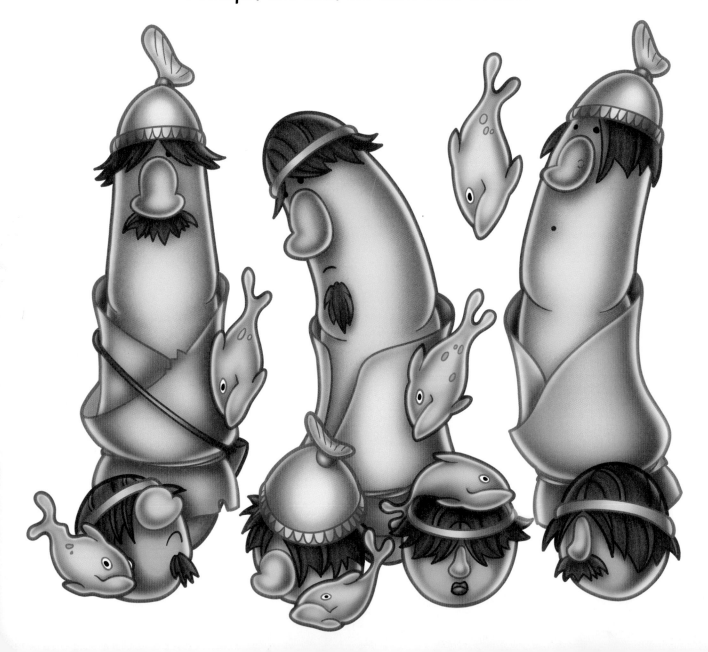

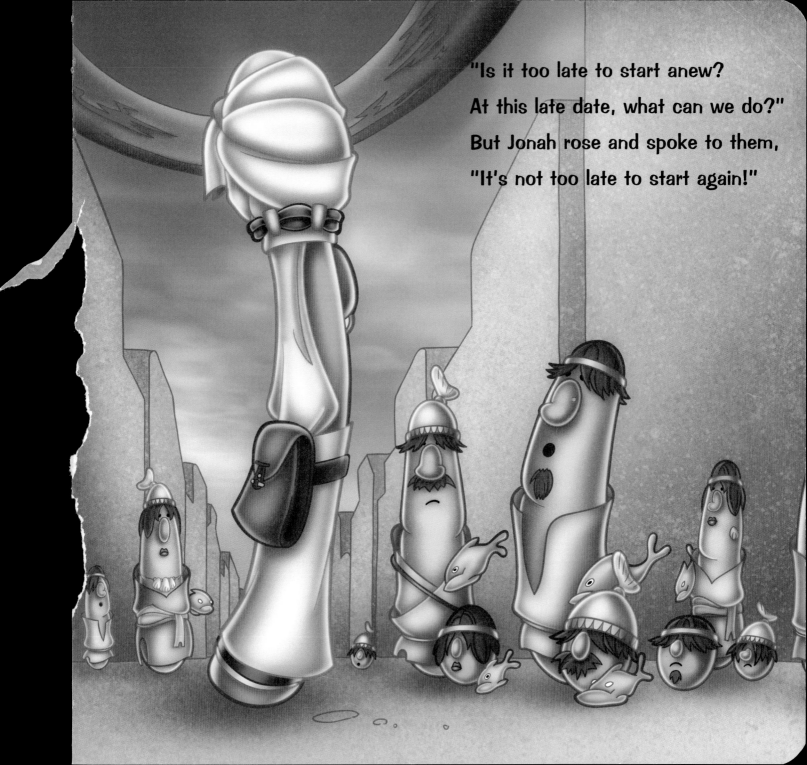

"Is it too late to start anew?
At this late date, what can we do?"
But Jonah rose and spoke to them,
"It's not too late to start again!"

You can do it! Yes, you can! God's got a starting-over plan!
A second chance is what you need! Then you can start again, indeed!"

This filled the Ninevites with praise,
And so they vowed to change their ways,

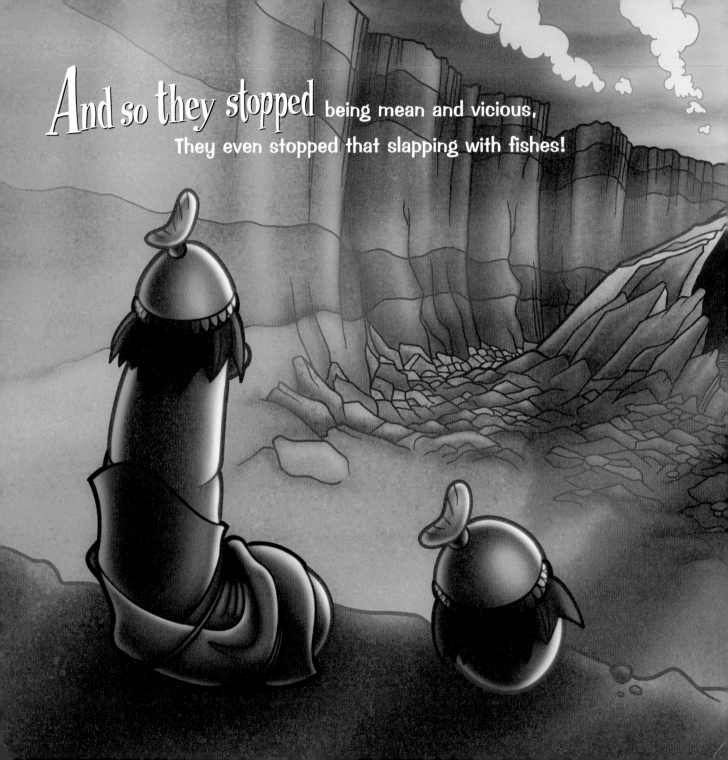

And so they stopped being mean and vicious,
They even stopped that slapping with fishes!

If **YOU** do wrong, just say a prayer, and know that God is always there.
God never closes any doors. A second chance can now be **YOURS**.